# THE BEAR
# THAT HEARD
# CRYING

# THE BEAR THAT HEARD CRYING

*Natalie Kinsey-Warnock*
*and Helen Kinsey*
*Illustrated by Ted Rand*

SCHOLASTIC INC.
New York  Toronto  London  Auckland  Sydney

## AUTHOR'S NOTE

THE STORY of Sarah Whitcher is true. Sarah was only three years old when she got lost in the woods near Warren, New Hampshire, in June 1783. For four days, people from surrounding towns looked for her and just when the search was to be called off, Mr. Heath showed up and found her according to his dream.

When she was older, Sarah wrote down what she remembered of those days in the woods and the "big black dog" that found her. Many of the searchers wrote down their accounts also. It was these accounts that my sister, Helen, found in an old history of Warren, New Hampshire, while doing geneological research, and we went together to research the area where the Whitchers lived and where Sarah got lost.

This story is all the more special to me, because Sarah Whitcher was my great-great-great-great-great aunt. Her brother, Jeremiah, born in 1790, seven years after Sarah was lost, was my great-great-great-great grandfather.

No record is given as to what happened to the bear. I hope it lived a long and contented life.

*Natalie Kinsey-Warnock*

ON A WARM afternoon in June 1783, Sarah Whitcher got lost in the woods.

The day began like any other Sunday. No axes rang in the great pine woods because Sundays were a day of rest. A church hadn't been built yet on Pine Hill, so Papa, Joseph, Reuben, John, Betty, and Sarah, who was three years old, sat under the trees near their cabin while Mama read from the Bible.

"It's a beautiful day," Papa said to Mama, after dinner. "Let's walk to the Summit and see Chase and Hannah's new baby."

Sarah loved her Uncle Chase. He took her for walks in the woods and showed her bobcat tracks and fox dens, and once he took her to a hollow tree on Pine Hill that bees had filled with honey.

Mama put on her hat and she and Papa walked along the path into the woods. Sarah ran after them.

"I'm coming, too," she said.

"No, Sarah," Mama said. "It is too far for you to walk. You must stay at home with Betty and your brothers."

Sarah meant to be a good girl, but she wanted to see Uncle Chase and the new baby. So when Mama and Papa were out of sight, Sarah followed them.

She walked along Berry Brook. Brook trout swam in the deep green pools. High above her head, squirrels and gray jays scolded her. The trees grew so tall Sarah was sure they touched the sky.

I'll pick some flowers for Aunt Hannah, Sarah thought.

She was so busy looking for wildflowers that she wandered from the path into the deep woods.

She ate some wild strawberries and picked bunches of wood sorrel and dogtooth violets. A bobcat leaped over a log, scaring her, but he bounded past, chasing a rabbit.

Sarah walked on and on. Blackberry brambles scratched her hands and feet, and her legs were tired. I hope Papa and Mama come back soon, she thought, but Mama and Papa never came.

Darkness crept into the woods. The wind moaned through the trees like a crying animal. It made Sarah want to cry just to hear it.

She was too tired to walk anymore, so she sat on a mossy rock. She tried to be brave, but the woods seemed too big and too dark, and before she knew it, she was crying. She was hungry, and so tired, and she wanted to go home. What was keeping Mama and Papa so long?

Sarah heard branches cracking. She held her breath, listening. Something was crashing through the bushes, coming right at her.

A big black head poked through the bushes. Two black eyes looked at Sarah, and Sarah laughed. A big black dog has found me, she thought. He will show me the way home.

But it wasn't a dog that had found Sarah. It was a shaggy bear, as black as the night.

Sarah was glad to see the dog. Now she didn't feel so lonely. She patted his long brown nose and hugged him around the neck. The bear sniffed her face, then licked the strawberry juice from her hands, and the blood from her feet where the blackberry brambles had scratched her.

Sarah put her head on his shoulder, and the bear lay down beside her. Sarah snuggled into his thick warm fur. Papa and Mama will find me tomorrow, she thought, and then she fell asleep.

Back on the path, Mama and Papa were hurrying home. The children ran to greet them.

"Why did you leave Sarah up at Uncle Chase's?" Reuben asked.

"We did not leave her," Papa said. "We told her to stay at home with you."

"She hasn't been here all day!" Joseph cried. "We thought she had gone with you."

Mama's face turned white.

"Sarah is lost in the woods!" she cried.

Reuben grabbed the dinner horn and bolted for the woods. Mama ran to the Richardsons, their nearest neighbors, for help.

Other neighbors came. They shouted into the forest and built great fires hoping Sarah would see them. But Sarah didn't come back.

No one slept that night. Papa searched the woods in the dark. Mama sat by the open door all night, listening for Sarah.

In the morning, the news of the lost child traveled over mountains and valleys. All who heard it left their farms and hurried to Pine Hill. Some of the neighbors left their oxen yoked in the fields. Joseph Patch came with his long-barreled gun.

For three days, people searched for Sarah, through the darkest forest to Moosehillock Mountain, up to Oak Falls, and all along the path up to the Oliverian River where it tumbled out of the dark ravines along Black Mountain. But every night, they returned, hungry, tired, and discouraged because they had not found Sarah.

Late in the afternoon, one of the men burst out of the woods. He was breathing hard from running.

"I found Sarah's footprints near Berry Brook," he said. "But there were bear tracks next to them."

"She's been torn to pieces!" several in the crowd said.

Mama covered her face with her hands. The children looked at each other but didn't say a word.

"She will never be found," someone said. "We might as well give up."

"No!" said Mama, lifting her head. "Don't give up yet. Please look for her one more day."

The searchers were sure that the bear had killed Sarah, but no one wanted to say that to Mama, so they agreed to look one more day. But no one expected to find Sarah.

At daylight, the woods filled again with people. Mrs. Richardson stayed at the Whitcher cabin to bake a bushel of beans to feed the searchers. She was busy by the fire when she heard a knock at the door. A man stood there. He was dusty and tired and looked as if he had walked a great distance.

"My name's Heath," he said. "I can find the child."

Just then, Joseph Patch came into the clearing.

"What makes you think you can find her when we've looked for four days with no luck?" he said.

"Last evening, I heard that a little girl was lost," Mr. Heath said. "Three times during the night I dreamed I found her lying under a great pine tree where the path crosses Berry Brook. A bear was guarding her."

"I don't know as I believe it," Mr. Patch said, "but I'll take you along the path."

When the path crossed Berry Brook, Mr. Heath stopped. He looked around, then plunged through the bushes. Mr. Patch followed him, and there was Sarah, sleeping under a large pine tree, just as Mr. Heath said she would be. There were bear tracks all around her.

Sarah opened her eyes and sat up.

"I want to go to Mama," she said.

Joseph Patch fired his gun into the air, then picked her up and carried her home. Everyone they met ran ahead of them, shouting and waving their hats. They all talked about Mr. Heath's wonderful dream.

Papa and Mama heard the shot and hurried back to the cabin. They heard the shouts of the crowd, "John! Sarah! We have found her!" and then they saw Sarah in Joseph Patch's arms.

Mama fainted. Papa couldn't say a word,
but he smoked his pipe as hard as he could.
Joseph, Reuben, and John whooped and
hollered, and Betty clapped her hands.
"Sarah's home! Sarah's home!" she sang.

"She must be famished, poor thing," Mrs. Richardson said, and hurried to fix her some soup.

Papa carried Sarah into the house. He sat in the rocker, holding her tight.

"Did you see anyone in the woods?" Papa asked her.

"A big black dog stayed with me every night," Sarah said. "He was friendly and his fur was warm."

Papa looked at Mama, and Mama looked at Papa, and no one told Sarah that the large black dog had been a bear.

Never had such a feast been prepared! Mrs. Richardson brought out her pans of baked beans and the women made venison stew, hasty pudding, and corn bread with honey.

*To Harris*
N.K.W.

*To my granddaughter, Sierra Jean Schaller*
T.R.

ISBN 0-590-02420-5

Text copyright © 1993 by Natalie Kinsey-Warnock and Helen Kinsey.
Illustrations copyright © 1993 by Ted Rand. All rights reserved.
Published by Scholastic Inc., 555 Broadway, New York, NY 10012,
by arrangement with Cobblehill Books, an affiliate of Dutton Children's Books,
a division of Penguin Books USA Inc.

Typography by Kathleen Westray

12 11 10 9 8 7 6 5 4 3 2 1                    8 9/9 0 1 2 3/0

Printed in the U.S.A.                    08

First Scholastic printing, January 1998

Papa said a prayer of thanksgiving and everyone sang. All the men blew horns and fired their guns over and over until all the powder on Pine Hill was used up, so great was the joy that Sarah was found.